Dogged Doggerel

FIFTY-TWO POEMS
by
A.B. Lawrence III

+

A WORLD WAR I REMEMBRANCE

AND

THREE CHILDREN'S STORIES

DOGGONEIT

What is more lovable than a Dog-
Eared book with its dust cover long gone
Its once bright pages smudged by the fog
Of time and just being held for so long
Because the words within keep calling
You, back to your future with a song
That reminds you of your first falling
In love when nothing much could go wrong

Pictured on the front cover is Stewart, a wonderful rescue dog that
recently joined the family.

© Arthur B. Lawrence III 2014
All Rights Reserved
Grandfather's Imprint
ISBN 13: 978-1502324252

WITH GRATITUDE:

To Ba Rea for her help and patience in bringing this book to publication. Ba has written and illustrated several books and is particularly known for her work on the monarch butterfly. For more on her butterfly and bug books visit her web site at (http://www.basrelief.org)

To Larry Berger for his help, encouragement, friendship and sharing of his writing over these many years. Larry has published a book of poems titled **Longing**. His book is available through Amazon Books.

To my son, Bart for his help in editing and willingness to let sleeping dogs lie.

To my bride for a lifetime of indulgence. Here is the answer to your question ----

Dogged Doggerel

CONTENTS

FIFTY-TWO POEMS

IN REMEMBRANCE OF WWI UPON ITS CENTENNIAL

THREE CHILDREN'S STORIES

BY WAY OF INTRODUCTION

For much of my life I have enjoyed playing with words, mostly in a poetic format that could be best described as dogged doggerel.

Traditional poetry relies heavily on predefined structure and the simplest form of that is found in syllable count and a rhyming pattern. It is in that field of word play that I usually find myself.

This book holds a collection of poems, each containing one line borrowed and attributed. For most of the poems in this book, I have taken a synectic approach in their development. Here is how it works. First I read a poem and excerpt a line that catches my eye. Sometime later I revisit that line and title it with the first thing that comes to mind. Then the game begins. The challenge is to fill in the blank space between the title and the borrowed line. The prize is the finished poem.

Poetry is a wonderful substitute for games like scrabble and crossword puzzles. Poetry is akin to painting with words, it hones your observational acuity, it draws upon your life's experiences and the cost is manageable for most.

It is sincerely hoped that the reader will seek out the referenced authors' poetry and discover the many shared concerns and life experiences that live through their work. The easiest way to access the attributed author's poem is to visit the internet or, preferably, buy one of the referenced anthologies noted.

Also included is a poetic remembrance to the soldiers of World War I. This year is the centennial of the war to end all wars. This remembrance brings to life how poetry played a very real part in the lives of the men who fought that war.

Finally, I have included three story poems for children. Friends and family have long asked when I will expose one of these stories to the light of the day, so here are three. It just seemed necessary!

And so, with apologies to the likes of Shakespeare, Burns, and Kipling I offer this: It is said that a murder (of the English language) will be seen differently by each witness and with each passing minute the recounting will be shaded by the hands of time. Therefore, I plea --- no crime intended!

REFERENCED ANTHOLOGIES

Keillor, Garrison. *Good Poems*. Penguin Books, 2003.

Blaisdell, Bob. *Elizabethan Poetry: An Anthology.* Dover Thrift Edition, 2005.

Negri, Paul. *English Victorian Poetry: An Anthology.* Dover Thrift Edition, 1998.

Blaisdell, Bob. *Imagist Poetry: An Anthology.* Dover Thrift Edition. 2011.

Poetry: The Essential Collection of Classic Works for the Nook. Press Shop NOOK Press eBooks, 2013.

FIFTY-TWO POEMS

SUNSET REFLECTIONS

How many times have we sat by the water's edge
Listening to shore birds as they fly into the night
Watching the tide rise then fall, leaving a new ledge
For tomorrow's children to dig into, some might
Even discover their future in a handful
Of sand and currents flowing and sun sets glowing
But we, we will sit here, long, and just be grateful
You with a glass of wine, I, a bourbon, knowing
That many live "through blank and oblivious years"*
And some will die having never seen the wonder
Of the sun's last light drawing in the dark of night
Or seen lightning dance from cloud to cloud with thunder
Singing in counterpoint to the surf landing light
Upon the sand, soothing the mind with the grandeur
Of God's creation, the random chaos that brings
Man and beast to their knees and then, in time, levels
All things, yet, in the light of this, nature still sings
So must we, in the face of all that bedevils

*Life, Anna Laetitia Barbauld, 1743 - 1825

ONE LINE

Seldom is the first line the best
The heart and soul beats in the rest
The rhyme and the meter hold you
Tight to the words, many or few
And together they sing a song
That can last for a lifetime long
But one line can make a difference
Whether direct or by inference
And cause the heart and soul to fly
And ask the mind to wonder why
Or lead you down a garden way
And help you know another day
And "if you strike a thorn or rose"*
Or find yourself where nothing grows
Think for yourself a poem to be
As grand as what you wish to see
But if the first line is the best
Still take the time to read the rest

*Keep A-Goin'!, Frank Lebby Stanton, 1857 - 1827

OARS SHIPPED

The first pull of the oar straightens the boat
Firm, eager, graceful as it wants to float
Hand over hand with oars balanced and matched
With each stroke the mind becomes more detached
The warm glow of the dock light becomes more
Distant and we grow closer as the shore
Dissolves into dark and darker places
As the night slowly, gently embraces
Us and graces us with its heavenly
Mantle till all about is gravenly
Set before us and we let our boat glide
Where no one can see us and we can't hide
From the naked beauty that is now ours
"In thoughts sublime that pierce the night like stars"*
We lay back, listening to the lullaby
Of night sounds and the only passerby
Is a loon that occasionally calls out
With a hoot and holler that is, no doubt
One of the grandest reports that nature
Provides, but that is not the nights feature
Performance, there is the bullfrog's bellow
The sky blinking in bright whites and yellow
Planets calling the soul to celebrate
In silence, leaving no voice to denigrate
This --- is a latitude and longitude

And moment that gives the mind quietude
The saints would speak a new beatitude
And the world could know a new attitude
Even ancient gods and philosophers
And the Adolfs and the Alexanders
Could find their peace in this guideboat
And it might just hold them all and still float

*The Choir Before Us, George Eliot, 1819 - 1880

MOVE OVER BUD

The bar turned to end in a dark corner
There he sat looking more like a mourner
Than the newly married man that he was
Why? You might ask and he'd answer, because
Then turn his glass slowly around, slowly
His olive eyes looking sad and wholly
Absent of feeling, they say that his wife
Is perfect as is their house and their life
Some take issue with the size of their lot
But they are not happy with what they've got
And never will be, according to John
Who is always flush with opinions on
Everything, until the closing hour
When the sweet smell and bloom of the flower
Is washed away with the swill of the night
But not the corner sitter, he remains
His remains are like the scars and stains
On the barroom floor, there but never seen
Lost to the cracks of the great in-between

But then "the wretch concentred all in self "*
To the very end he ordered Top Shelf
And this he did without apology
As was noted in a fine eulogy
Spoken from that dark corner of the bar
Where no will ever know who you are

*Love Of Country from "The Lay of the Last Minstrel," Sir
   Walter Scott, 1771 - 1832

A COMMANDING VIEW

His words bellowed with clarity and song
"It matters not how deep intrenched the wrong"*
His nostrils flared betraying his deep passion
The cut of his clothes belayed his fashion
A man who commanded your attention!
He had a presence beyond convention
The world was swayed and swooned for his vision
Clearly, justice for all was his mission
And every man-mother-and-child knew this
That they too had felt the seductive kiss
Of the devil among them, but what wrong?
In the end it did not matter, his song
And dance was enough to keep them spinning
While the world stood still, the moon watched, grinning

*Be Strong, Be Strong, We Are Not Here To Play (Hymn),
Maltby D. Babcock, 1853 - 1901

NIOBE SLAID

Never so fine a fence has been made
Than the fence made by Niobe Slaid
She set each post with exactitude
The rails held firm to their latitude
The slats were spaced with such precision
That all could see her perfect vision
Frost and folly could not diminish
This fence that never did she finish
There were miles and miles of fence she built
On land she bought like a patchwork quilt
Acre by acre she fenced it in
Then, she'd sit alone with such a grin
Everyone knew she was satisfied
And too, she sat with deserved pride
She sat alone with her great divide
With good reason to be gratified
People would stop, ask why, or what is it
But not a one would stop and visit
And she would reply: "A fence my friend
A fence complete that's without an end
The beginning, you see, is on my land
The rest you'll find is perfectly planned"
To one and all it was very clear
She held her fence to be very dear
No Sawyer could hope to paint its slats

No Penrod could wish to rest his fats
And the homes behind this great white line
Soon were empty and wanting to pine
For the days when children ran about
And greetings were given with a shout
Hey, how are you, and what do you know
I see your corn has started to grow
The woodlots grew thick, the fields grew thin
But to the end the old gal would grin
For the fence she'd made was truly great
But, "It matters not how strait the gate"*
Or how true the line or fresh the paint
The memory of this will fast grow faint
And disappear with the rub of time
Leaving naught but this, a little rhyme

*Invictus , William Ernst Healy, 1849 – 1903

INEXPLICABLE

Words, so many words floating on the wind
Words, oh how they sail inexplicably
About my brain; calmly, excitedly
They lean and they tumble, they flounce and slant
Rhyme, and they will do what words really can't
Vowels and consonants, syllables upon
Syllables, build until the early dawn
Then through the day, with joyous assonance
They hop, skip and jump, they prance and they dance
They race up stairways in heavenly bliss
They rest on the lip as sweet as a kiss
They travel "through the corridors of time"*
And they never alone commit a crime
They comfort the living and praise the dead
And they nourish the mind when it's unfed
And desires to eat some food for thought
With words so rare that they cannot be bought
Some words get caught in a grand diagram
Others wax poetic or just amscram
To the place where that pig and poker live
And none should enter unless they would give
Their mother tongue to the devil's dungeon
Where ghouls and fools will wantonly bludgeon
Words, till they're but a whisper in the wind

*The Day is Gone, Henry Wadsworth Longfellow, 1807 - 1889

THE CHAR MAID

The char maid turned to her child and spoke these words, kindly
"Don't deal in lies" for they are like a bed left unmade
But then, what child does not believe in the truth, blindly
Until they have made their own bed and there slept and played
Seen the piper come and go, lived to love, others
Days and nights unfold and reveal the twisted, knotted
Folds and furrows plowed into the bed of our druthers
Brothers and sisters all, and so, all are besotted

* If, Rudyard Kipling, 1865 - 1936

TUG HILL STILL

It's hard to know how far "far" is until
You've been there, but once there, there is a still
Quiet and inviting solitude, shared
By few for, in this day, most will run scared
At the thought of fields full of the black fly
And the freshet where many fine fish die
Or roads closed in by snow banks ten feet high
Early fall days that cause the ducks to fly
South, and north winds that whistle a winter
Tune, too soon, and call the ax to splinter
The ash, beech and maple into cord wood
That has to last past the spring, spring is Good-
God awful when the frost goes out and mud
Sucks your packs off, or you hear a dull thud
When your oil pan lands on a big old stone
And you're miles from anywhere and alone
So delightfully alone and you can
Look up and see the clouds racing the man
In the moon as the stars play hide and seek
While the waters roil and boil in Fish Creek
Then a branch slaps you, sharply, in the cheek
You swear at Mother Nature, take a leak
Laugh, smile, and know that you will never die
And go to heaven. Why'd you even try
When you've found heaven on earth and have walked

The long walk back and in the moonlight, talked
To the stars, listened to the wind's chatter
Danced with the trees and let the mud splatter
Where it may, then sat at Aggies's table
And dined till you were no longer able
To talk of tying flies and fish and hunting
Fourth of July porches hung with bunting
Children chasing fireflies in the field
Memories of cards dealt and hands revealed
And a long forgotten story, revealed
Over a late night pour of aged whisky
And when the day is over and the night
Has fallen nigh, you know that all is right
As you leave, once again, into the still
Passing "the little grey church on the hill"*
Thinking that you should stop some day and sit
Where others have sat, sung and didn't quit
When the snow drifts were still eye high in May
Or the fall hadn't seen a good drying day
And the oldest boy was called off to war
Never to return to that hallowed door
And sing hallelujah for the land he
Loved and all that he left for you and me

*No Title, Mathew Arnold, 1822 – 1888

PEARLS OF INNOCENCE

We are born complete in our innocence
"Yet in the maddening maze of things"* to come
The good and evil song of dissonance
Becomes the sounding and the pounding drum
That soon is the rag-tag parade of life
That we all march in, with banners unfurled
Melding love and hate into a song rife
With tragedy and full of hope unpearled

*The Eternal Goodness, John S. Wittier, 1807 - 1892

THE FOGGY FOGGY HUE

At so many times in nature spaces
And so many ways in people places
I have felt the fullness of the hour
I have seen the wind touching a flower
And smelt the dampening dew upon a fern
Burn away while I watch the blossom turn
To face the daylight with all its gleaming
Then cast a shadow for midday dreaming
That soon will fade and then fill the darkness
With shades of grey and still greyer closeness
That becomes the dark of the darkest night
Then, as we are wont and are bold to say
We come together "on the trysting day"*
Where time is past moving, and still, and quiet
Yet each moment is replete with riot
And there we embrace the maddening crowd
That is us, and for this nature has bowed

*Horatius, Thomas Barington Macaulay, 1800 - 1859

KNOCKING, KNOCK, KNOCKING

He knocked on the door of inequities
And there saw dancing his iniquities
The music playing was disquieting
And yet begged him to join the rioting
A sweet song of seduction, timpani
In his temples, drowning the symphony
Of sensibility, a little show
Of horrors that will give him cause to know
Well, "the question she asks, oh why, oh when"*
Then pleads -- does the everyman know this den?

*Sea Fever, John Mansfield, 1878 - 1967

SHROUDS AND CLOUDS

The capstan's been turned, the anchor, secure
The course has been plotted, it's true and sure
Now a brisk "wind blows and the vessel goes"*
Out to a sea where a tempest soon grows
The deck is fast wetted and then awash
While down in the bilge some water does slosh
The shrouds are a whistling a salty tune
The sails are reefed and it was none too soon
The wind was now blowing a full force 10
And there stood the captain where few have been
His hand now held firmly that ships great wheel
He sailed his vessel through a danger, real
With a gentle hand and he sailed wave to wave
And kept that fine craft from a watery grave
When the wind slackened and the sky turned blue
He smiled at the wind the stars and the crew
Lucky was he to be one with the sea
That much he knew for a sailor was he

* All is Well, Arthur Hugh Clough, 1819 – 1861

YESTERDAYS
Heade this

Yes, I can remember my youth
Like it was yesterday
But in truth
Yesterday was a bit foggy

We played and then you
stayed

OH LAUDY!
You and I had a plan a day
But it was like rolling
In the hay
Looking for that needle is fun
When all is done and said
You're my hun

"Eternity's a Five Year Plan"*

SO

Whenyoucandoitnow

Hit the fan
With the proverbial feces
And>#%*you'll<&%#find$@*the^#!*human---------------
kind species
Frenetic   all over
the place
Watch watching, gob gobbling
Pretty face
People who turn the world ugly
Have their own five year plan
Live smugly

And have never seen a haystack
Waiting for the return
Of lovers

*Eternity's a Five Year Plan, #52 100 selected poems, E.E.Cummings,
1894 - 1962

20

EMBRACE OUR LAND

To look across the fruited plain
And gaze upon purple mountains
Majesty! The vast bounding main
That embraces our land, fountains
Of inspiring thoughts springing
Forth, visions grand, lush, breathtaking
Canyons and caverns, brooks singing
Lamenting the crass heartbreaking
Discards of our life, trinkets, trash
Troubled souls marring the wonders
Of the world, reticent and rash
We are wanton in our blunders
We will stand, someday, and we'll pray
"Here where embattled farmers stood"*
Now yearning for a better day
Embittered, we will see the good
In walking a bridge to nowhere
Seeking something left unaltered
By these cloven hands that reap, tear
Rend and leave nothing un-haltered

* *Concord Hym, Ralph Waldo Emerson, 1803 - 1882*

THE TASTE OF LIFE

The taste of mother's milk was once sublime
A novel of high acclaim cost a dime
For a nickel you got a candy bar
And a dollar could put gas in your car
Time was once measured in days and in years
And things had buttons, levers, and gears
The specialist was someone who could do
What you could do, only better, and you
Well you and I, we just throw it away
And who takes the time to write and to pray
Remember when clouds were black, white and grey
Now clouds are full of digitized matter
Raining tweets by the masters of prater
What of "the things that are more excellent"*
A sentence complete or a well turned phrase
A thought contemplated for days and days
A letter written then posted by hand
A song sung, standing by a baby grand
A flower picked by the edge of a stream
The time taken to enjoy a daydream
Or follow a butterfly through a field
And not consider that our fate is sealed
Is the taste of life but sweet and sour
And time a place that can't spare an hour

*The Things That Are Most Excellent, William Watson,
   1858 - 1935

HAT MAN DO

"Hats off"*
Thanks Jack for all you did for US
PT109, all the fuss
All great men die and some, sadly
You lived your life well and badly
At times, but then, you were mostly
Human, like US, so intensely
Did you live, that you had to die
Too soon, the world was fast to cry
And slow to learn the lesson lady
Death leaves behind, in dark, shady
Places, where fear is found riding
A headless horse while deriding
All that could have been and never
Will be for ever and ever
Hats off to you my man, hats off
As one and all our hats we doff
No more because you set the style
And dared to stand hatless and smile
And let the sun shine on your face
So that we can be free of grace
Good manners and go bare-headed
Into a world where the dreaded
Word cancer travels on sunbeams
And burns away all hopes and dreams
And so our hats we doff

*The Flag Goes By, Henry Holcome Benett, 1863 - 1924

10 ON THE RICHTER SCALE

The man sat peacefully, wiling away the day
Thinking he would live, "yes, forever and a day"*
He was comforted by sounds of swift song birds
And the music of his lover's most tender words
Each kiss was richer than the wine that passed their lips
And a Sistine moment was the touch of their fingertips
So sure were they that this was the love of ages
That they did not care for the wisdom of sages
Past or future fancies that liven the hour
Did not engage them but a delicate flower
Before their eyes captured the beauty of all time
They saw the song birds fly and heard the church bells chime
As they embraced and closed their eyes to the world to
See the inner beauty of love and know that two
Can be one and feel the earth tremble beneath them
And it did, and it did and then it consumed them!

*The Children's Hour, Henry Wadsworth Longfellow, 1807 - 1882

STRAWBERRY HILL
(so they can remember too)

When we were young and innocent of consequence
The children would lead us to the strawberry field
Out beyond the barn and the crabapple tree
Those were the days when time could pass and leave us be
The living and the loving were a compact sealed
With a kiss, morning and evening, our confidence
Grew in the fields and valleys surrounding our home
As the flora and fauna soon became divine
From the teasing of a cricket to the prodding
Of a toad while we watched butterflies deciding
Which way to go in a blizzard of dandelion
Snow, there was a season for that too, you could roam
For miles, hushed but for the sound of your skies gliding
Over nature's great hiding of spring time delights
The weight of the child on your back is a comfort
For most journeys cannot be so shared an effort
Fast becomes the measure of every task, the nights
Called you out to embrace the heavens, clouds riding
On a sea of stars, fireflies dancing, a breeze
Whistling, trees complaining, the windows rattling, heat
Bellowing from the furnace, the sounds of children
Sleeping, without the cares of the world to burden
Them and their little feet that have not known defeat
Will run to the edge of the bed and try to tease

Us from our slumber and the wonder of dreaming
Of our children "kissed by strawberries on the hill"*
But it is never so for most or very long
For all - children - who have not heard the joyful song
Of nature we should dream less and together fill
Their valleys with strawberries wild, wet and gleaming

* *The Bare Boy, John Greenlief Whittier 1807 - 1892*

AS THE WORLD TURNS

As the world turns and churns and burns a path
Across the heavens, heaven knows what wrath
Is caused for those who live in its shadow
What portent might arise and foreshadow
Some dire consequence in our passing
There we might see grand armies amassing
Massive edifices built to honor
Us as the one, the great, grand abettor
Of a stone arguing with babbling
Brooks that converge into a bubbling
Cauldron that will some day produce living
Breathing, things deceiving, things believing
What would "the man of independent mind"*
Think and what would he do if he could find
Darkness in light, peace in cacophony
Stillness in storm, pleasure in harmony
Any being living in a shadow cast
By the likes of us would have to move fast
Or be buried in the dust of ages
Layer upon layer of outrages

*A man's a man for a' that, By Robert Burns, 1759 - 1796

GIFTS THAT GROW WITH EVERY LIVING THING

The old man took a walk to the far side of wild
Bent but not broken he stood there and smiled
There at the edge of the middle of a forest
Deep where a lesser heart would fail the test
Of standing alone in an unfamiliar land
Where silent sounds are hard to understand
And inviting sweet smells can mask a bitter fruit
There is a rustle in the brush, an owl's hoot
Who-who is heard and a lone snake unwinds its coil
Death whispers in wood and moldering soil
A mouse runs under some new fallen leaves
The night will bring a killing frost, here nothing grieves
The old man wonders who will be the first
He knows that it is wonder that whets man's great thirst
And too, that leads all things great and small, astray
But he, being neither great or very small this day
Stands still like the bird of prey, mind agile
Darting like the mouse, cunning like the snake, fragile
As the late fawn that does not notice him
Warm memories of his youth, now seem ever so dim
For some here the night is sure to be grim
A coyote's howl is heard from beyond the hill
And he remembers the thrill of the kill
He claps his gnarled hands twice and you can guess the rest
For he knows that "gifts that grow are the best"*

*Plant A Tree, Lucy Larcom, 1807 - 1882

A ROADSIDE WARRIOR

Sitting by the roadside without a goober pea
Sitting by the roadside for all the world to see
Sitting by the roadside with hat in hand and bag
And nothing more to hold but hollow cheeks that sag
Standing by the roadside he turns to take a pee
Standing by the roadside for all the world to see
Standing by the roadside his clothes are such a mess
That you and he might just agree that more is less
Squatting by the roadside he defecates right there
Squatting by the roadside for all the world to glare
Squatting by the roadside 'tis all he has to share
That and nothing more than a bit of passing air
Laying by the roadside one day he finally dies
Laying by the roadside there is no one who cries
Laying by the roadside, for now, and then he's gone
Gone to where we'll never know, gone without a song
Kneeling by the roadside for all the world to see
Kneeling by the roadside I pray for you and me
Kneeling by the roadside I see a buzzard fly
Why oh why, "there, but for the grace of God go I"*

*No Title, John Bradford, 1510 – 1555

TWO OLD CROWS

What kind of understanding is this
We live, we love, we laugh and then kiss
It all away, the good and the bad
But the indifferent that is where mad
Men gather, it's the great middle ground
Where idle and addled thoughts are found
All this is known and so little more
This I know from watching the birds soar
From seeing an ant carry its treasure
Watching an elephant at leisure
Caring kindly for an orphaned calf
Sharing the pleasure of a child's laugh
Today there are two old crows sitting
On a fence, eye to eye, there, cawing
If black-faced they'd have us guffawing
Today they're just sitting on a fence
And heaven only knows why or whence
They came, where they go may not matter
But watch them preen and hear them prater
And you can't help but smile at the thought
Of vaudeville and what Two Old Crows brought
To the parlor on the Victrola
While we sipped rum and coke-a-cola
And spoke of the shared humanity
Of it all and the insanity

Of how we look over our shoulder
Now when we speak about things bolder
Than baseball or the color of red
Then I saw, soaring, way overhead
Vultures, circling without a sound
"Lifting the soul from the common ground"*
Soaring like eagles circling the sun
Waiting to feast on what we have done

*Gradatim, Josiah Gilbert Holland, 1819 - 1881

JOCUND PLACES

The woods are a fine place for wanderlust
To take hold, it is in trees you can trust
Trees and streams and fields where shadows are cast
On ferns and flowers and memories fast
And thus, forever embraced, can roam free
Not bound by the horizons of the sea
Or caverns of a cityscape that bind
One to the hum-drum of the daily grind
"Far from the madding crowd's ignoble strife"*
Where you can touch, taste, smell, feel and know life
For what it is and is not, more or less
The sum and total without mankind's mess
It is people and their maddening ways
That can foul the most glorious of days
One harsh and thoughtless word can shatter joy
And leave life to be lived without a ploy
But words and woods share not a common ground
And nature has no madness that I've found

*Elegy Written In a Country Church-yard, Thomas Gray,
1716 - 1771

AH, POMONA
59th & 5th
NYC

Ah, Pomona you wet and wonderful thing
Drenched in your aquas world, you sing
Your song as the world of tits and glitz
Passes by, and there I see a lady sits
Where once "a woman sat in unwomanly rags"*
Sorting and shifting some twenty odd bags
She handled her treasure as if it were gold
Her face and her hands were etched and so old
Looking, and her hair was thinning and unkept
Her face was streaked as if she had long wept
Her dress for the summer was of burlap and shag
And she smelled a smell that could make you gag
Her legs were scarred and wizened by sun and time
And she spoke to herself with the voice of a mime
Her shoes I think once had been worn by a gent
And she counted her pennies, cent by cent
No beggar was she, at least not that hour
And by her side there rested one flower
But not one person gave her a glance
Then who, I thought, would take that chance
And the passersby cut a wide berth
As if, by chance, she had soiled the earth
Then, for a moment, I looked in her eye

And saw a vision of youth waiting to die
I blinked, and she got up to go
And why, I knew I would never know
She left her flower right where it lay
And two lovers sat down and started to play
They pulled at the petals of a forget-me-not
And I, well I, never forgot

* *The Song of The Shirt, Thomas Hood , 1799 – 1845*

Note: Pomona was the Roman goddess of abundance and stands at the top of the fountain in front of the Plaza Hotel, NYC, NY.

THE PHILOSOPHICAL PHIOLOSOPHERS AND
THEIR PHANTASMAGORICAL BARN DANCE

I have to be absolutely honest
With you, I was an uninvited guest
Still, I was welcome, even though they knew
That absolute honesty must eschew
Reality, yet, it was a very
Real walk in the woods, and a bit scary
Too, when I came upon that dark clearing
A stark moonlit place, a place worth fearing
For it held a barn that held more firmly
Voices of the past, an anomaly
That was me, for I had lost my Latin
(Even though I was raised in Manhattan)
And Greek and French could not be forgotten
Having not been learned, I stood besotten
For there, at the far end of the barn, stood
Apollo, the Apollo, I mean good
God he was grand, as he played and sang
While a dozen odd men, long in the fang
Seemed to move about in a trance, a dance
Du renard, keen of eye, sly of foot, glance
Dance, peer, shuffle, gaze, prance, stare, all drifting
They moved about the barn, never lifting
A finger, mumbling intelligibly
All knowing but not seeing it, yet strangely
I knew what they were seeking, and the point

Of it, I knew I stood in counterpoint
To their ageless brilliance, their timeless presence
Their extraordinary effervescence
When they saw me standing there, pointing at
A needle in a haystack, that was that
The be all to end all, the point of it
Yet not, for Plato was the first to sit
Aristotle handed him the needle
Head first, eye to eye, it appeared regal
In his hands, he turned it, all watched closely
And all were intent upon it, mostly
Because it was Aristotle who had
Deferred and passed it on, he looked quite sad
I thought, but did not know how long his quest
Had been with the camel and eye thing, rest
Assured, he was not reticent as time
Went on, speaking in a common tongue, I'm
Pleased to report that English had become
The link language, no more French, though, for some
A lyric word or two would pass their lips
But, for the most part, these were seen as slips
Of courtesy and accommodation
Noted with lifting brows, incantations
And platitudes, at times, followed with ease
Here, there seemed to be no effort to please
Words were the weapon of choice, victory
Was found in silence, where all history
Becomes hysterical, a force beyond

Blind belief or the waving of a wand
Nietzsche seemed hell bent on conjugating
The movement of time in space, debating
The relevance of the fifth dimension
The needle, not worthy of his mention
In the flickering light of kerosene
Lamps, nothing seemed to be as it had been
Moment to moment these magnificent
Minds mastered points of view, munificent
In their declinations, impenitent
Of their postulations, ever intent
That is, except Will Rogers, he would look
My way and smile, Confucius had a book
A compendium of thought that could fit
Every construct, that's the beauty of it
After all, everything is a construct
That will inevitably destruct
By self or another initiative
Here, argument was the imperative
The saintly Thomas doubted everyone
Epicurus needled him for the fun
Of it, the needle, of course was stoic
And Zeno thought it to be heroic
For it could mend and draw blood with sameness
Of purpose, still, there was a shamelessness
That Locke defined as the cold, steely way
That a needle with thread could make the day
For all dandies and damsels of distress

Yet just one prick might cause them to undress
I did not see Protagoras that night
But his presence, there, was felt, wrong or right
Base and erudite words flew, heavenly
Words rolled from tongues savagely, hauntingly
And, at times, a sense of satisfaction
Was reveled, however, interaction
Decorum and clarity were preserved
Though Descartes' geometry soon immured
Him to the back of the barn, elegance
Alone was not enough for this fine dance
And dance, dance alone should suffice, Freddy
Ayer called this the rational and ready
Solution, the philosophical dance
The eternal question, the devil's prance
Spinoza took a spin at it, the dance
I mean, he saw it more as a fine lance
That could violate the most tender heart
Or raw heel, then, from that barn's darkest part
I heard a different voice, "Once I thought,
But falsely thought"* and it taught
Me the danger of knowing", a putto
Emerged carrying a shield with the motto
IGNORAUTIA EST BEATITUDINIS**
And then he stopped and smiled and took a piss

Then, and this is the most amazing thing
Harry Houdini was there, emerging
From the shadows, he stood before Plato
Harry was a man whose only credo
Was et inveniant veritatem effugere***
And so, he acted without constraint, the
Gathered illuminati then mounted
The needle's head and danced on, undaunted

I wish I could tell you more of that night
They tell me I must have had a bad fright
This I know, I will have a lot to learn
They say that my memory may return
Fully, someday, for there were other guests
There, they say I was found running west
On Route 66 wearing only my
Driving hat and cravat, the how and why
Of it all seem as distant as my past
But there is one thing, here, that may just cast
Some light on all of this, see, over there
A piece of straw, look, stuck in my hat, there!
If you'd just loosen these straps I could show
You, please, damn it, there's so much more to know

Epilogue

This article appeared in the local newspaper:

"MAN LAST SEEN RIDING A YELLOW HORSE"

A man that arrived at the Devil's Ridge Regional Hospital a fortnight ago, suffering from trauma induced amnesia, has disappeared. Also missing is the attending nurse, Xanthippe (Ann) Lamprocles. Ann had recently moved to the Valley of the Saints and lived with her grandfather in a rented farm house a two step down the road from the Joneses of Hillview Heights Road. It is said that she rode a yellow horse to work, rain or shine. This may be nothing more than a big lie for such an ignoble thing would be most unfortunate. A fellow nurse reportedly overheard Ann ask the attending physician, Dr. Syntax, about when the patient would be well enough to travel. It is believed that Ann's grandfather had gone to visit some old friends earlier in the week. The authorities would like to speak with anyone having more information regarding these individuals. Please contact the police at Pennsylvania 6 5000.

* FROM THE BOOK; ELIZABETHAN POETRY, ANOMY-
    NOUS C. 1595-1608

**ignorance is bliss
***escape and find the truth

AT THE EDGE OF IT

As the huddled muddled masses waited
One man stood at the shore with breath bated
"What matter," he thought, "if I stand alone"*
He hesitated then picked up his phone
And threw it far into a breaking wave
The crowd shouted, that's no way to behave
Then hunkered down to a collective frown
In the mist they could see him drop his shoes
Into the water, they could see him loose
Everything, then walk away with a smile
Mile after mile after mile with a smile
Knowing that the rising tide would come in
Soon he would have a new life to begin
Far from the maddening crowd left behind
Left to wonder if he had lost his mind
Too, who's to say how a man is defined
Far, far away from the work-a-day grind

* Waiting, John Borroughs, 1837 - 1921

HARDLY

"Hardly a man is now alive"*
Who remembers that famous day
And year" –It was in 65
So very many had to die
Near 700,000 did
One country indivisible
Held in bondage, chained to its ways
Humanity immutable
A lot more had reason to cry
Then there's 1789
14 July when the French had
Their say, and on cake they did dine
With faces powdered and perfumed
Blankly staring at the future
Forever, the genteel life doomed
And what blood was given to sign
King John, fifteen June twelve fifteen
Words, just words you say, benign
They say the terrible reigns were
Shifted from a goat to an ass
But only the whip can be sure
Says the boss man on the chain gang
There ain't no better way to say
Unce uz getz de hang oz de slang
As today we butcher our words

To prove the meaning of free speech
Well, I think it's all for the birds
Soon the vultures will be picking
Picking and pecking at our bones
And then there is the knife sticking
Deep into the back of Caesar
Julius, of course, the ides of March
He could have been an old geezer
So too the boys at Pearl Harbor
Boys and girls at Hiroshima
Leave us with dates that fester
In the deep recesses of our
Minds-eye dates like 9/11
We will forget the year and our
Children's children won't remember
The tears and years and years of fear
Fear! Let's hope they don't remember

*Paul Reveres Ride, H. Wadsworth, 1807 - 1882

LADY LUCK

It matters not if it's early or late
"I knock unbidden, once at every gate"*
Whispered the sprightly little old lady
At every door, closed or ajar, maybe
Twice but seldom thrice will you hear the tap
Tap, tap of lady luck calling, the rap
That waits for no man, and wants no excuse
All dreams hang nightly in a tightening noose
Choked by the light of day, suffocated
By the weight of all who hesitated

* *Opportunity, John J. Ingalls, 1833-1900*

MOUNTAIN WHY

From a brief encounter at Castle Rock

Why does she do it, climb all those mountains
She could have sipped Pernod by the fountains
Of Paris or bathed her feet in the baths
Of Rome but she chose to roam other paths
Rough and rugged courses that took her deep
Into the woods, she'd run, walk and creep
Over craggy rocks, slippery, moss shrouded
Magnificent vistas, sometimes clouded
Over and over again, up and back
She climbed the 46 Adirondack
High peaks three times and the Green Mountains too
The Appalachian Trail wore out her shoe
But not her, not even New Hampshire's White
Mountains with Mount Washington's soaring height
Mountains, none were daunting, all are vaulting
As she reached for the heights, steps un-halting
Wanting to be "betwixt the beautiful"*
Rocks, lichen, shadow brushed, bent tree, artful
Hand that guides us, makes us all that we are
For a minute we stood and saw so far

*Knee Deep in June, James W. Riley, 1899 - 1916

SORRY

Long he sat with a silly grin
He never knew where to begin
Just getting up was hard to do
He might have to learn something new
Or find his way without asking
That or maybe multitasking
Walking and chewing bubble gum
Was overwhelming, it was dumb
Walking was hard but harder still
Were the steps and going uphill
The grade was always too steep
His pace was a crawl, then a creep
Life was going nowhere but fast
Time, that, he thought he could outlast
Yes, he was the eternal man
His motto was, maybe I can
"Humanity with all its fears
With all its hope of future years"*
You could see it in his beady
Eyes, shifting, drifting and greedy
It makes me feel sorry to think
He can't outrun the kitchen sink

*The building of the ship (of state), Henry Wadsworth Longfellow,
    1807 - 1882

TRILLIUM TRAILS

That early flower of spring
Is a wondrous thing
It's found on trodden trail
And in the morning vale
It's by the old beech tree
There's one, there's two, then three
But one alone is fine, so fine
For this is, its time
Fragile before the seasons change
How strange
Yet common to all
The seasons as they fall
This coming and going
Of life and the knowing
This flower will cling to craggy slopes
And places where life holds no hopes
But "nothing is fare or good
Alone,"* this is understood
As you step in a bog
Or brush a rotting log

That shades this little flower
And lets you rest an hour
With your head on a mossy bed
And so the quick and the dead
Together
Are one forever

Each and All, Ralph Waldo Emerson, 1803-1882

THE LOGICAL WAY

Justice and jail, bucket and box, marriage
Sublime mayhem, the horse and the carriage
The horseless carriage, the chance encounter
The perfect date, dry toast, bread and butter
All hands on deck, the words that you mutter
The garden sundial, the atomic clock
The sound of a babbling brook, hard rock
A hard rock and its shadow, the shadow
On a lonely wall, on the floor, waiting
Waiting on, someone listening, what you hear
Washington DC and Los Angeles
All for one, one for all, nobles oblige
So this is the way of a world, you say
"That was built in such a logical way"*
Pray and look and see in the grand design
Perfection and know that we'll all be fine
In the random nature of all things dear
There is joy and love, there is loss and fear

*"The Deacon's Masterpiece" or "The One Horse Shay,"
Oliver Wendell Holmes, 1809 - 1882

NIGHT LIGHTS

The old man walked into the room and turned
The night light on, night after night it burned
For the little children around the world
The boys with snakes and girls with their hair curled
Who slumber with ease and sugar plumb dreams
And never fear or hear the midnight screams
Of Malaman, that bedroom beast that prowls
And moans and groans from his most wretched bowels
Then, with a fearsome roar and teeth not white
He tells a tale of all that is not right
He stirs the aged and even the young
By remembering all that is left undone
He can paint pictures with vivid colors
Of what we do to ourselves and others
He can sing a tune with a raspy voice
A song that will end with now it's your choice
He'll make you recall a long forgot pain
And cause you to fear the loss of a gain
He can wear away the walls we erect
And cause our beliefs to become suspect
As visions once sharp are, so soon, clouded
He causes hope to go cold and shrouded
In the dim light of despair and the scare
Of falling, falling and nobody's there
To catch you or care if a beastly beast

Will chase you down and have you for a feast
In dreams of dark and silent sophistry
or
"A protest that is also a prophecy"*
Malaman and old men embrace the night
But old men know that to turn on the Light
That shows the way to the comforting arms
Of a mother, it's the best of all charms
That ward off the fears and demons of night
And lets little children sleep, snug and tight

*The Man With A Hoe, Edwin Markham, 1852 - 1940

NOTHING WRIGHT

Frankly speaking, some men and their craft

Leave one to wonder if they are daft

Who'd build a house on a waterfall

Or make a room that's absent a wall

Why would a space that's made for living

Be cold and hard and unforgiving

The arrogance of self has no place

In a home for a home without grace

Is better left for nature to down

And out the light that so dimly glowed

And scarred the land where nature once flowed

Where I encounter "a wall so blank"*

That "my shadow I thank" I also thank

That the hand of time will wipe away

The mark of man where the angels play

*The Song of The Shirt, Thomas Hood, 1799 - 1845

HIS ABUNDANCE

Before him spread the lay of his land
Lush fields and woods with a house so grand
A jetty held his ship resting proud
The skies above had nary a cloud
His halls were hung with pictures perfect
And his wardrobe is the most select
He sleeps at night on a feather bed
With but one thought resting in his head
And the image of a man so gaunt
This; "before I knew the woes of want"*
I met my needs without excesses
Or the applause greeting successes
I slept with a youthful visage near
And I gave no thought to loss or fear

*The Song of The Shirt, Thomas Hood, 1799 - 1845

LIFE IS FULL

Life is full of fits and starts
Growing pains and body parts
That fall and fail over time
As we seek a life sublime
But in the quest to achieve
And stand for what you believe
Take the pauses life gives you
Use them to learn something new
Learn it well and learn it through
It will better all you do
Do it well and do it full
Fall not to the shortcut's pull
"Find some knowledge at each pause"*
Not for why but just because

*The Blessed D Damozel, Dante G. Rossetti, 1828 – 1882

BUT FOR THE TREES

Yes, "Only God can make a tree"*
But man alone can make it be
Something more than twigs and ash
Or rendered into just cold cash
I've seen the artist make by hand
A purest form that is so grand
I've seen the trees that give a place
For words to live and speak with grace
I've seen a cooper bend a board
For wine that soon will praise the Lord
I've seen a shipwright work a plank
For boats to sail not hank for hank
And when the drought and draft is done
And too the sailor's race that's won
God and man can thank the tree
And a muse, though fool he may be

*TREES, Joyce Kilmer, 1886-1918

NOT FOR THE WIND

I look upon a cold and dreary day
And see "these varied winds forget their way"*
The damp sets in and chills the bone and breast
A duck alone will see this day the best
A duck it is that swims before my eye
A duck with chicks too small to think or cry
They swim as one close by their mother's back
The water near turns dark, then nearly black
A distant strike of lightening catches my eye
Yet calmly still the ducks swim on and by
Then, the wind cuts and curves upon the lake
As if the gods are angry as they rake
Then a chick appears from within the reeds
While far away the mother duck still leads
Her other chicks along the water's edge
Past fallen trees and a gray rocky ledge
This smallest duck then cranes its neck and calls
As all about the wind still whips and mauls
And then I see the duck and chicks return
It's not for the wind I feel my eyes burn

*Columbus, Joaquin Miller 1833-1913

WHO EVER ASKS

For whom do they speak
"But to do or die"*
They that are too weak
To lift but an eye
What reason do they
Have, or need to be
On life's stage, today
Their eyes are a plea
For gentle passage
Their hunger in life
Gone, too the visage
Death without a knife
Bloody or report
Loud, to tell the end
So quietly, old sport
This is your last bend
On the road to hell
Or, Heaven only
Knows if all is well
And peace is comely

*The charge of the light brigade / Tennyson 1809-1982

A Reflection on the night before of my father's death. He had served
as a lieutenant in the Paratroop Rangers during WW II

ILL WINDS BLOWING

The world is swept by a gentle breeze
To the gods of old it's barely a tease
But man can make the freshest air
Into a storm so harsh and rare
That all about scream in pain
And then parade, proud and vain
As work and war make man humble
Before the gods they kneel and mumble
Prayers of peace for what won't be
For it is there for all to see
"Of marble men and maidens over wrought"*
It is in this storm that they are caught

* Ode On a Grecian Urn, John Keats 1795 - 1821

WHEN LIFE IS BEST

The man stood, old, cold, on a grey
Midsummer's day with clouds affray
An early frost threatens the night
A damp mist holds his memories
Tight to his breast where he carries
His life's great love, still young at heart
A love that wants to dance and part
With all the aches and pain that time
Has rested on him, but the shine
Is gone from his eyes, and he cries
In the deepest dark of the night
Silent tears of joy for the great
Great gift that he has been given
From him, this cannot be riven
he thought
A child will think that life is best
"When rocked to rest on mother's breast"*
but
The old man knows the best of life
Bears the edge of a well-worn knife
Honed on stone and stropped with leather
Long held and sheathed close together

*The Cloud, Percy B. Shelley, 1792 - 1822

ONCE AND AGAIN

The old grey mare stood at the edge of the field and He
Well He stood knee deep in the weeds where once tall cotton
Stood for something much, much more than money in the banks
His Mama and Pa had told him just how life will be
They had leaned the hard way, life's truths not soon forgotten
You start, pick a ninny worth of cotton, then give thanks
Praise the Lord that you're white and get a share of the crop
And then grow old with dark, dark leathered skin like Grandpa
Did, so did his Pa and Great and Great Great Grandpa do this
But how could they have known that death would soon put a stop
To this mind-numbing life that they lived, like an old saw
He has never forgotten what she said and her kiss
"Say yessum to the ladies and yesure to the men"*
She had just said all this to his brothers and sisters
But why did she return and kiss his feverish forehead
Why'd he have to get sick and miss the county fair, then
Why, all this in the land of hurricanes and twisters
Why, he thought, did the car crash and leave them all so dead
Something really, really big could have taken them all
But this left him in an orphanage, very alone
And now, some eighty years removed from the high cotton
Fields of his youth he listens to a mocking bird call
He smiles, thanks God for all this and the dog with a bone
His wife is gone now, kids have moved on, what's forgotten
Is not important and soon what's important is not

Remembered by anyone, not even the postman
Who has retired and still walks by this fallow field
Gives the old grey a carrot and the dog gets a lot
Of ear rubs while he sits there and watches the old man
And wonders where he came from, always looking well-heeled
But he looks too old, his skin is too light for this place
He's seen him before, out there, but they've never spoken
There has always been too much distance between them
He knew that old men from this place were bent and their face
Would be dark and appear etched with tears, most look broken
And old before their time, it's from this land all things stem
Nature's pruning is often cruel, seemingly mindless
Thought the postman, besides, no ones ever met the Man
Who's let this good land rest idle for some sixty years
The postman left this place without a name or address
He walked, bent, knowing that he'd done all that a man can
Still his face was etched by years of smiles and years of tears

The old man in the field whistled and the horse came
To his side, along with the dog they walked up the hill
An hour later they reached a fence and the far side
Of his property, a small well-kept house had a name
Different than his! His aunt's son, Will Devine, lived there still
In lieu of rent they cared for his dog, a horse to ride

And a vegetable plot, all the things he couldn't have
Living in the city where he had made his fortune
Good fortune had smiled on him and work had made him rich
Beyond his dreams, but in life there is no greater salve
Than the knowing smile of family because much too soon
It's all over and then you find your eternal niche

*Just For Christmas, Eugene Field, 1850 – 1895

CLEAR SAILING

He sat at the short end of a long bar
Muddling his drink, not seeing very far
Beyond his nose, he puts his glasses down
He rubs his eyes as he lets his thoughts drown
His world has become a sea of worry
Each storm has its own torment and fury
Now, his sail's luff with the wind on his bow
One hand holds the rail, but he can't see how
In irons, now he must break free of all this
Duty calls, then he goes to take a piss
He returns and again he takes his stance
He looks in the mirror, just a brief glance
The smoke of ages clouds his lonely view
For all that has past he can't see the new
He knows "there comes a moment to decide"*
He looks again but there's nowhere to hide
He then pushes away a glass half full
And leaves with the tide on its daily pull

*The Present Crisis, James Russell Lowell, 1819-1891

COBWEBS PUSHED ASIDE

The old man opens an attic trunk

Full of linen and letters and junk

Treasures of a lifetime put away

To be held again one lonely day

For

"Oh, the years are many, the years are long

But the little toy friends are true"*

He

Will remember the battles fought

The ladies chased and the ladies caught

And he will recall life's ups and downs

Millions and millions of smiles and frowns

But oh to hold a soldier of lead

One in uniform of faded red

One that has shared the battles of youth

A soldier in arms that knows the truth

That little boys bright and little boys blue

Will grow to be men and do what boys do

*Little Boy Blue, Eugene Field, 1850-1895

WITH SNOW

There is with snow a grand design
And not of making, yours or mine
For with the winds that blow at night
There are designs that will delight
Waves will rest on fields awaking
As branches bend close to breaking
Leaving the woods and fields to be
A welcome place and fine to see
And in a hollow there I spot
One lone leaf that fall forgot
It stands in contrast sharp and true
To the tree where it once was new
And there a drift has made a bed
For a doe and fawn just fed
Then as the sun breaks through a cloud
A spruce grouse beats its drum so proud
And all about glistens and gleams
You know that this is how God dreams
Like the "frolic architecture
Of the snow"* shadows all nature
Devolving all that will matter
With nature's caress and prater

*The Snowstorm, Ralph Waldo Emerson, 1803 - 1882

65

TO SPEAK OF

"The terrible grumble, and rumble and roar"* of war
Is lame and tame, a shame for it's all that comes before

THE BLOOD AND GORE

The greed and need and glory's steed that opens the sore
That pesters and festers and beckons our young to war

AND THE FOREVERMORE

* *Sheridan's Ride, Thomas B. Read , 1822-1872*

SUNRISE ∞ SUNSET

We see the beauty of the day
Dissolve in the ocean and say
Now the sun belongs to someone
Else, we think that the world has spun
For us alone, painted the skies
For us alone, and the green eyes
Of a lover, mine have seen this
And the stars appear and a kiss
Given for every twinkling
Light is like a summer sprinkling
Of love on the life that we share
So it is, with all that is good
Very little is understood
Less is known, much is felt in love
The light and dark the push, pull, shove
Quietly, "and it must follow
As the night the day,"* the hollow
And the robust, all else is thunder
Smoke and mirrors, song and dance, wonder

* *From Polonius' advice to Lasrtes, William Shakespeare, 1564 -*
  1616

SUNG SONGS SUNG

Sung songs sung without the meter of time
Sung without the grace of pathos and rhyme
Have but the gaiety of a whistle
In the wind and the prick of a thistle
And yet the thistle has a singular
Beauty, coarse, vibrant and spectacular
As sure as a whistle can make the day
Of one who is lost and is want to say
That their days are bleak and their nights are cold
But this, we all know without being told
"Ye wot no man so wise is born that keeps
His wisdom constantly"* unless he sleeps
With one eye open; a foot on the ground
Hand on heaven; hand on hell and the sound
Yes, the sound of sirens serenading
Tugging on the heart strings of time, invading
The sensibilities, rendering all
Cold, calculating ready for the fall
And when the fall comes it is they that stand
Ready to reap the wind, able to grasp
The cold harsh reality, look the asp
In the eye, smile and choke the life from all
That would dare stand in the way of the fall

*Ballad Of The Gibert, FRANCOIS VILLON, 1460

THE GREEN-EYED LADY

It is not time that binds us to this earthly space
For we are free to live and die and stand and face
Life as it is with all its warts and snarly sorts
The bugaboos and ballyhoos and their cohorts
That will dance daily on all God-given delights
With a little luck the sun will shine and nights
Will fill with stars, glistening and gleaming stars
And fond memories of marching bands and stars and bars
And streets that are filled with people that smile and look
You in the eye, for to see and be seen in the book
Of life is far better than to find that your page
Is but a footnote that is never turned to, sage
Thoughts are no substitute for clarity, action
And charity in all things, save the attraction
Of idly "thinking of the brilliant eyes and green
And purple hue"* that beckons boys to the obscene
Pleasures that the barker hawks at the county fair
Midway, for that is where boys become men and stare
At girls who learn that the value of temptation
Is worth more than the simple act of redemption

*The Spider And The Fly, Mary Howitt, 1799 – 1888

YEARS AGO

People of her ilk
Lived in feathers and silk
They came out
And for what purpose there was no doubt
God, family, country and tea
Oh! And a place in the country or by the sea
Would do
But they didn't have to do
Anything that didn't suit
Them and the blue suit
And white gloves kept them apart
Their heart
Was in the right place
But their face
Was always put on, on guard
They were always waiting to play their card
Bridging the gap between then and now
Doing the bidding of others
Pleasing their mothers
Pouring tea in the afternoon
Having a nip of gin, a bit too soon
Savoring the blood that runs in their veins
Bound together by invisible chains
Time passes; there are so many minutes to kill
Someone bids one no trump, all is still

You can hear their plea and know their pain
Surly someone will say "I shall not live in vain!"*
But no
At five they each have somewhere to go
At seven-thirty they have somewhere to be
Conversing lightly
Dinner at eight-fifteen
And they all know the in-between

* If I Can Stop One Heart From Breaking, Emily Dickinson,
   1830-1886

MERCY, MERCY

Mercy, mercy cried the old fool looking pained
His shirt tails pulled and his old tie, very stained
Just for living one thinks that he should be blamed
But, "the quality of mercy is not strained"*
Nor is freedom from fear ever to be gained
By avoiding the chance, Given, to be kind
But then watch, he will pay you no-never-mind
Watch him sit, slowly, then see that he's half blind
And then watch him wipe a silver fork, three tined
On his yellowed cuff, and too the knife and spoon
Then, from paper bag, he pulls a half moon
Cake, cake you think, and it's only noon
You see him pause, then whistle a happy tune
As he places a candle between the light side
And the dark side of the moon, with pride
For some, you think, life must be a bumpy ride
He looks at you, you blush, but you can not hide
He offers you the empty seat across the table
You feel compelled but wonder, are you able
His hand gestures, graciously, and the table
Waits, his face has the markings of a fable
It wants to tell a story too sad to hear
Could it be, his life, drowned in urine and beer
Yes, or maybe drugs, the earring in his ear
Tells a lot about a man, isn't it queer

How the unknowing can bring forth such fright
Visceral, mind bending, keep you up at night
You sitting there, now wouldn't that be a sight
Someone might see and the whole damn world would know!
You think, all of this in a flash, and it's so
So very, very reasonable to go
After all, you are a reasoned man and know
You are known by the company you keep, the low
And high, you call to a friend across the way
You have the perfect excuse to walk away
There is something that holds you here on this day
The candle is lit. Is it that that holds sway?

* "Mercy" from the Merchant of Venice, Shakespeare, 1564 - 1616

In Remembrance of WWI
Upon Its Centennial

I CAN REMEMBER

I can remember standing at a crossroad
With men of stature, bearing a heavy load
Their chests all ablaze with the colors of war
Not just the last one but the several before
The war to end all war!

Their families stood near, as they had in the past
The sun is high, but the shadow that they cast
Is long, for long ago they stepped to the fore
Marching spritely and rightly as those before
No man could ask for more!

We cannot know the battles others have fought
But we can see in their eyes what war has wrought
The loss of life and limb, love and so much more
And for some it's clear there's still an open sore
But not of blood and gore!

I look up; the sky is blue, the fields are gold
And it is humbling to stand among the bold
Each with a crimson poppy on their lapel
Each is closer to heaven and knowing hell
Each, a story to tell!

I look back at the Norman church we came from
Where I sat touching a Knight whose days were done
My hand resting gently on his stone-cold feet

His story long forgotten, his grave replete
Death is so, so complete!

A chestnut horse moves across an open field
With no mud and blood spattered scars here, unhealed
The quiet recalls no battle drum or shell
Blast that rends the flesh and leaves death's heavy smell
Yes cry; war is hell!

We bury our dead at sea and hallowed ground
The taps are played then we hear death's silent sound
"Between the crosses, row on row"* we may stand
Listening we hear the silence of the land
Can we understand?

Still we have our grand parades with fife and drum
And still, on we fight for death is deaf and dumb
So numb we are, now, to the parade of life
That we no longer see death as close and rife
Death's a wanton wife!

I remember sitting on my grandfather's
Uniformed shoulders, like so many others
I watched and wondered as the boys all marched by
And I watched and wondered -- why do old men cry?
Why? So many cried!

Today I open an envelope with words that read
But do not tell of how many, there, would bleed

Poppy from Flanders Field
　　　(Vimy Ridge)
Liut C.P. Franchot Oct 1917

This flower now faded and fragile holds the tears,
Hope and dreams that can't be held with buttressed weirs
All these many years!

*In Flanders Fields, Lieutenant Colonel John McCrae, MD,
(1872-1918)*

The Lieut McCrae could not have known of the awful
carnage that would ensue in 1917 at Vimy Ridge.
His poem was penned in December of 1915.

In the fall of 1917, my grandfather Charles Pascal Franchot
went to France. He was aid-de-camp to a Major General
O'Ryan and they were on a tour of inspection with the
New York National Guard. The Guard was mobilized the
following spring. He wrote many letters home from France.
Little could be said of the war because all correspondence
was censored, though, he frequently commented on his fine
horse and requested cigars and sweets. Today, this pressed
flower still speaks loudly for those lost and the times he
lived in.   .

In this year, 2011, the last American veteran of WWI died!

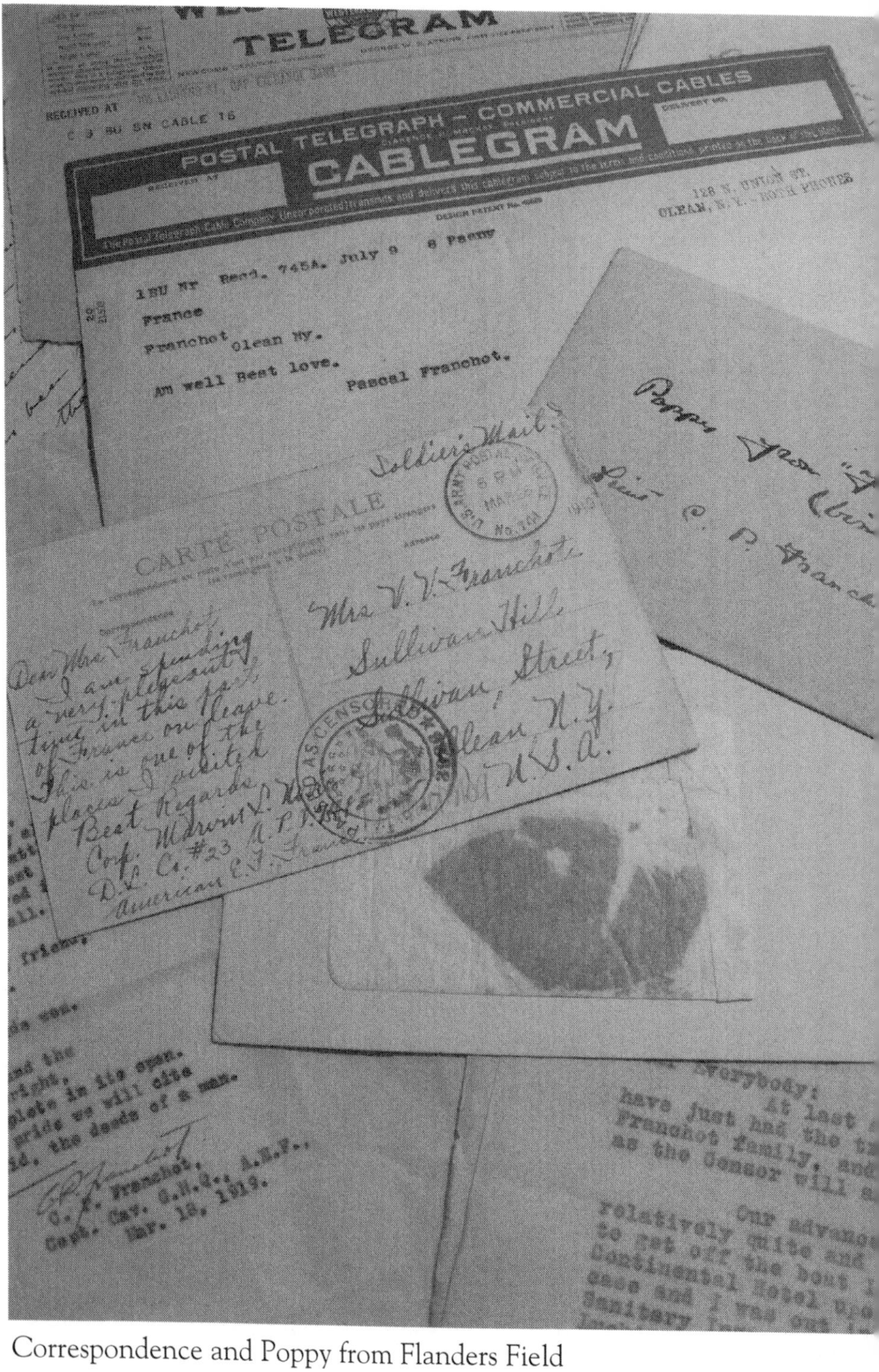

Correspondence and Poppy from Flanders Field

The following is a poem penned by my grandfather, C. P. Franchot, in memoriam of a friend. It was printed in a newspaper and read by a cousin and comrade in arms who was a Brigadier General, USA. Unfortunately his signature is beyond my ability to decipher. I have included the text of his response and the text of the original poem because they exemplify how poetry was well received and expressed without reservation during times of war.

To Major David McK. Peterson

American Ace: formerly of Lafayette Escadrille, Distinguished Service Cross; Croix de Guerre (two citations to order of army); killed in
Aeroplane accident at Daytona Fla.

Quiet but forceful, kind but strong.
Faithful in study, careful in act.
Brave in action, despairing the wrong
Capable always and gifted with tact;

Valorous, generous, giving your best.
Loved by your comrades, respected by all.
But death that you played with in battle and test.
Beckoned at last and you've answered its call.

France looses in you a chivalrous friend.
America's loss – a glorious son.
Honored by both before the end.
By medals of valor for gratitude won.
Though youth was still yours and the future was bright.

Your lifetime a full one, complete in its span.
Deep though our grief, with pride we will cite.
Your achievements so splendid, the deeds of a man.

Signature
C.P. Franchot
Capt. Cav.G.H.Q., A.E.F.
March. 18, 1919

Response:

AMERICAN EXPEDITIONARY FORCES

Tours (APO 717)   6 April, 1919

Capt. C.P. Franchot,

G.H.Q., A.E.F

A.P.O. 706.

Dear Cousin Pascal:

Your poem to David, which was published in the Herald, caught my eye last week. It is splendid as well as a well-deserved tribute, and I wish to thank you very much for it. I am sure his father and Charlotte will also appreciate it greatly.

I have not heard about the accident to know how it came about, but assume from what little I have seen that something probably went wrong
with the machinery when he was too close to the earth to straighten out.

Trusting our paths may cross again before long, I am,

Very sincerely
Signature
Brig. Gen., U.S.A.

THREE CHILDREN'S STORIES

MOORE CHRISTMAS

It was the night before Christmas*
When all through the house
All creatures were stirring
Yes, even the mouse

No stockings were hung
There was no chimney there
Our thoughts of St. Nicholas
Were just television fair

The children were watching
Not using their heads
All glued to the tube
And not in their beds

I in my night shirt
And mom in her gown
We had just settled in
For a long winter frown

When out in the yard
There was such a noise
I thought to myself
That must be the boys

I ran to the window
And threw up the sash
Which promptly came down
And broke with a crash

The street lights were lit
Casting shadows on snow
But no one was there
Now, where did they go

Then all of a sudden
What should appear
But a broken down sleigh
And eight tired reindeer

There was a little old man
Not lively or quick
I thought, could this be
Could it be St. Nick?

Sad as it was
He was not the same
For try as he did
He couldn't remember a name

Calling Crasher and Basher
Oh, Answer and Where Are You
Please Stumbles and Grumbles
Yes, Wander oh You Who

On top of the porch
On top of the wall
I thought for sure
One of them would fall

Not fleet of foot
Or sure of gait
This Christmas I fear
Will just have to wait

That's when I called out
To where the snow was high piled
Old man please come in
And he did and he smiled

He flopped in my chair
So tired, I'd say
"Exhausted", he said,
"I think I'll just stay"

He lit up his pipe
And started to smoke
Then said this to me
Now, this is no joke

"Christmas has gone
A thing of the past
Now it's tinsel and glitter
And toys that don't last"

"The children just watch
The video tube
Not for a minute
Do they come unglued"

"The Christmas trees stand
All plastic and bright
No feeling have they
It's a terrible sight"

"And stockings aren't hung
The same today
No songs are sung
And people don't pray"

"For gone are the mantles
And fires warm glow
Yes, gone are the chimneys
That down I could go"

"Oh, where has it gone
That Christmas joy
Where is the love
I gave each girl and boy"

Do you know, I thought,
St. Nicholas is right
Christmas has become
A frightful sight

It was then and there
That a thought came to me
All at once I knew
How Christmas could be

I ran to my attic
As quick as I could
And searched for the crèche
Yes, that would be good

I found it, in time
All covered with dust
And brought it downstairs
For I knew that I must

Off went the television
Out like a light
I set up the crèche
On that Christmas night

With candles all lit
And bows of green
To the children I read
From the Bible, this scene

Then by the table
Where the crèche was set out
The children were asked
To put their stockings about

St. Nicholas sat there
And loudly declared
"This is Christmas, it is,
It's Christmas we've shared"

He arose from my chair
And to the children said
It's time that I go
And you must go to bed

He went off to his sleigh
Where his reindeer assembled
So excited was I
I think that I trembled

With a jingle and a jangle
His sleigh left the ground
Never was heard
A more lovely sound

His cheeks were all rosy
Yes, Santa looked grand
As off he went
Spreading joy through the land

And later that night
I heard him return
With joy and love
To the candles we burn

Through the door ajar
So quietly he crept
With gifts for all
While the children slept

He ate the cookies
That we had left out
Yes, Santa had been there
Of that there was no doubt

The stockings were filled
With love and a toy
Then he scratched his head
And said, "Oh Joy!"

"Christmas is here
And to all good cheer!"
As off in his sleigh
He went up, up, and away

Proclaiming to all –
To all a goodnight!

*With apologies to Clement C. Moore, author of that timeless
Christmas story, The Night Before Christmas. His iconic story
was first published as a poem in 1823 and titled "A Visit from
St Nicholas."

MARBELLA

In the town of Marbella
I met this little fella
He was sitting with a little girl
Who held, it seemed, a little pearl

But this pearl turned out to be
Something very different, you see
It was, instead, a marble
With a story quite incredible

Extraordinary, I would say
And it started just this way
Long, long ago they made the very first one
A marble, and it was done just for fun

Then they made two and three
Each as pretty as can be
Then four, five, six, and seven
Eight, nine, ten, and eleven

With every one a shade of white
These marbles made a lovely sight
Though it was hard to have much fun
When each was like the other one

So one day they gave them colors
Like yellow, green, purple and others
Red, blue, and shades of black
Enough to fill more than a sack

Some had colors twisted and turned
Or colors in shapes that just aren't learned
Now and then one came out gray
But all were bright to make your day

They even made them in silver and gold
But those, I think, were hard to hold
For they are colors that seem to make
Just a bit more of give and take

Well, marbles became all the rage
A treasure for folks of every age
There were marbles that looked like cat eyes
While others had pictures and some held a surprise

No longer were they used just for play
Some were used, instead, for pay
While others were found perfectly selected
Then hidden away to be collected

There were games they made like an amazing maze
That people would play for days and days
Some went so fast that you could barely blink
Others were slow, but they made you think

There were games where marbles were tossed and flicked
And others where odds and evens are picked
Shooters were great and so were keepers
And you always had agates and cheaters

Well marbles came and some, they went
For this and that and even for rent
And all was fine until one day
The mayor decided he should have his way

He had found a marble so perfectly clear
It caused him once to shed a tear
He gave it a name; he called it a puree
But little did he know it would cause great worry

Now, many agreed, you understand
For truly this marble was very grand
So he issued an order to every one there
To bring all there marbles to the town square

And there in the square they could all discover
Just who had a puree, the best of all other
After they sorted and sifted them out
There were quite a number, of that there was no doubt

There were piles of marbles ever so high
To put one more on top you'd really have to try
They were all sorted out with the puree put first
And others behind until you got to the worst

When they had finished the mayor decided
That things had become a little lopsided
He said, you know, I think it would be fair
For all of us, now, to equally share

It didn't matter if some had been saved
While others found that had been carelessly laid
Yes, he had decided and that was all there was to it
Besides, he said, sooner or later someone would do it

Well, many about were a bit perplexed
And others, I would say, were just a bit vexed
No one was sure if the mayor was right
And some even said it would cause a big fight

Then someone noticed a pile over there
Where marbles were put with out any care
Some were broken chipped, or cracked
While others were worn or had colors they lacked

Though many were favorites or friends of old
They would all have to go, the town was told
And most agreed, indeed, indeed!
Besides, there were more than anyone could need

All agreed, that is, except for a very young lad
He raced through the crowd looking ever so mad
He ran to the pile, the one at the end
And picked up a marble, for it was his friend

A friend and companion through thick and thin
To hold it now just made him grin
And he held it high for all to see
But the mayor said, this cannot be

He grabbed the boy and shook him hard
The marble fell an inch, a foot, at least a yard
It bounced and bounced, then hit another
And that hit more and then, oh brother

There wasn't a marble sitting still
And they all started bouncing and rolling down the hill
At the bottom of the hill there was a sea
And everyone could see that was where they would be

People were slipping and sliding about
It was terribly funny, of that there was no doubt
Funny it was, and yet quite sad
For in the end they had lost all they had

And, as the last marble bounced into the sea
The people all wondered, what will ever be?
Will we ever have marbles about our land?
Will they ever be fine or just a bit grand?

For they had lost their marbles, that was for sure
Even the ones they had thought were so pure
Yes, all had been lost, all but one
For that boy kept a marble, just for fun

A TWO DOG NIGHT

It was one of those nights when you get into bed
And pull all of the blankets right over your head
Then both of your dogs lie down by your feet
One dog alone would not give enough heat

It was so cold that it could shiver a timber
You could chatter and shake and never get limber
The frost would freeze on the end of your nose
You couldn't get warm by curling your toes

Yes, it was one of those nights, it was Christmas Eve
And what happened to Santa was hard to believe
He had circled the world by the light of the moon
His toys were delivered and it was none too soon

He was on his way home when his sleigh hit a bump
Then he bounced right out and he landed with a thump
Santa's dog Brody had gone along for the ride
He also bounced out and landed by Santa's side

His dog shook the snow that covered his hair
Then looked at Santa who lay quietly there
He knew right then that he had to get help
But the best he could do was bark and yelp

He ran to the top of the nearest big hill
And started to bark into the night's dark chill
He barked and barked until his throat was soar
Then he barked until he could bark no more

Off in the distance he heard a reply
A wolf gave a howl; I'll give it a try
I'll pass on your message, Ahooo Ahooo
I'll do what I can. That's all I can do

Then you could hear a sharp, Arf Arf, Arf Arf!
It came from a Scottie wearing a scarf
He Arffed and Arffed as loud as he could
Until a sheep dog said he understood

The sheep dog went and he snapped and he snarled
A sound that could make sheep's wool all gnarled
In fact, I think he woke all of his sheep
For I am sure they were all sound asleep

But the message got through to a grand old poodle
Who was very smart but seldom used his noodle
Yes, poodles are clowns, of that there's no doubt
But he woofed and woofed till he was all woofed out

Next, a German shepherd out on a lark
His ears perked up and he heard the poodle's bark
He was quick to respond with quite a howl
Enough to open the eyes of an owl

Then out in a field you could hear a hound dog bay
Oh yes he'd heard the message of where Santa lay
The message was passed from this dog to that
The long and the tall, the thin and the fat

You could hear them all barking, ruff, ruff, ruff
Some dogs were happy and some dogs were gruff
Some dogs looked scruffy, others looked regal
And I know I heard one little beagle

And boxers and bulldogs and golden retrievers
You know, of course, there were doubters and believers
They all barked and barked as loud as they could
Hoping their message would be understood

All over the world you could hear the dogs barking
Of a place on a map where there was no marking
A place where Santa lay flat on the ground
With a big black dog, they hoped to be found

When the howling the and barking reached Santa's house
The first to hear it was Jehoshaphat, the mouse
He didn't know what all of the noise was about
So he went and woke Gretchen. He had to find out.

When Gretchen heard what the last dog said
She said, Oh dear, I must go get my sled
Santa's in trouble, he's out in the snow
I've got to hurry. I really must go!

He hooked up a sled, put a keg on his collar
Then Jehoshaphat gave a whoop and a holler
Off they went into the deep of the night
Hoping that Santa would be all right

They passed through some rain and a couple of blizzards
Where the snow swirled about like magical wizards
The snow drifted here, the snow drifted there
It was enough to cause a real bad scare

So Gretchen had to be very careful
And Jehoshaphat tried to be cheerful
Over field and forest, hill and valley
Not even once did they dilly-dally

When they came upon Santa they heard him call out
We're here, we're here, but how did you ever find out
Jehoshaphat replied, it's a long, long tail
We all pulled together, we didn't dare fail

They helped Santa Clause up onto the sled
And put a big hat on top of his head
They had to get Santa straight to his home
Santa was dizzy, they could hear him moan

It was Brody that then ran with the sleigh
Barking directions, "Up, up and away"
And away they all went, off to his house
Brody and Gretchen, Santa and even the mouse

They arrived safe and sound at Santa's house
And they all went to bed, even the mouse
They all slept together that Christmas night
Glad that everything had turned out all right

When they awoke to the morning's first light
Santa exclaimed, "It was a two dog night!"
Then he reached down to the end of his bed
He ruffled their hair and then Santa said

In life's little journeys, to have a friend
Can help smooth a bump and straighten a bend
So to one and all he said with good cheer
May your days be merry throughout the year
  (((MERRY CHRISTMAS)))

Made in the USA
Charleston, SC
11 November 2015